Seasons
of the Spirit

Inspiring
Women
to go deeper with God

Seasons
of the Spirit

Learning to live in the rhythms of grace

Jeannette Barwick and Beverley Shepherd

Foreword by Fiona Castle

Front cover image: Artville: Don Bishop

Concept development, editing, design and production by CWR

Printed in Finland by WS Bookwell

ISBN: 1-85345-329-3

Contents

Meet the Women at Waverley Team

Jeannette Barwick, founder of Waverley's Ministry to Women, has long been committed to helping women apply biblical principles to their lives and relationships. In 1987, the first event for women was held at Waverley Abbey House and over the years the heart of Waverley's teaching for women has been shared around the world through seminars, writing and audio-cassettes. Jeannette also teaches on temperament differences and coordinates Selwyn Hughes' worldwide ministry.

Beth Clark, the most senior member of the team, is a lady whose life is steeped in the Scriptures. Her Bible Study has been ongoing for nearly 30 years and her workshops on Bible Meditation at Women at Waverley weekends are greatly prized. She has endeared herself to all who know her, not only by her humility and prayerfulness, but also by her remarkable ability to establish rapport with people of all ages.

Beverley Shepherd has been a team member for over 10 years. She is involved in varied and demanding work as a training consultant. The encouraging and equipping of Christians in the workplace is one of her passions, and she is an associate speaker for the London Institute of Contemporary Christianity headed by Mark Greene. She brings to the team verve and vitality as well as depth of biblical understanding, and is especially appreciated for her ability to relate biblical truth to contemporary issues, particularly as they impact women.

Nicky-Sue Leonard is a a gifted teacher and a relative newcomer to the team, bringing to it her expertise and experience as a CWR-trained counsellor and facilitator of post-abortion workshops based on Christian principles. For a number of years she has co-ordinated women's events at Waverley and around the UK. Apart from an expanding role as a speaker at women's events, she is increasingly involved in teaching on CWR's counselling courses.

Foreword

At Waverley Abbey, CWR have been running weekends for women for many years, under the direction of Jeannette Barwick. She has always had a desire to inspire and encourage women to fulfil God's potential in their lives.

For all that feminism aspired to achieve, women, although more liberated into the workplace, do not seem to have gained more self-esteem. In fact, it seems to have made women more stressed than ever, trying to achieve perfection at work and in the home. Recent surveys suggest that the three highest causes of stress in women are work, family and home – and juggling all three. They also state that one in five women will have visited the doctor in the past month, with some sort of neurotic disorder. The most common symptoms are – fatigue, sleep problems, irritability, anxiety and depression.

With 70 per cent of women today working either full time or part time, what does this say about the quality of our current lifestyle? Modern technology was intended to provide human beings with more leisure time, but instead it has created a frantic desire to cram more and more into our already busy days, sometimes described as 'hurry sickness'!

Is this the way God intended us to live our lives? Selwyn Hughes once said, 'If we are too busy to stop and spend time praying and listening to God, we are busier than God intended!'

This latest book in the series of inspiring women, *Seasons of the Spirit*, co-written by Jeannette Barwick and Beverley Shepherd, sets out in a very creative way, to help women to order their lives, exposing the frantic and exhausting lifestyle which has become the 'norm' in society today.

It suggests, as in the book of Ecclesiastes, that 'there is a time for everything and a season for every activity under heaven' (Eccl. 3:1).

This includes stopping and resting! Furthermore I am delighted to note that the seasons are not referred to in terms of the seasons of our lives – which at my age, I find very depressing! Rather it points out opportunities in our hours, days and years, when we can be extremely active or retreat to rest and be quiet.

It is beautifully set out, to be used as a good read, as an individual Bible study or for group study.

Personally, I am so keen to do everything I can to build up self-esteem in women, that I am delighted to discover that *Seasons of the Spirit* is a book which I am sure will be a blessing to all who read it.

Fiona Castle
June 2004

Introduction

This book has grown out of two wonderful weekends of spiritual refreshing for women at Waverley Abbey House, CWR's ministry centre in Farnham, Surrey, on the theme of Seasons of the Spirit. The focus of our time together was to develop an awareness of what it means to move according to God's rhythm in our lives.

With the assurance that God has 'placed eternity in our hearts', we looked at the way God leads us into different phases in our lives – times of activity but also times of rest, times of fulfilment, but also times of deprivation and loss. Using the analogy of the natural seasons, spring, summer, autumn and winter, we called these phases 'seasons of the Spirit' because it is the Holy Spirit who leads us into each of these seasons, and the timing of this leading is God's. The seasons may be affected by life's circumstances, as some of the stories will illustrate, but have little to do with age.

To explore such a theme as this at any time in our lives can be incredibly helpful as a means of preparation for whatever may lie ahead. Naturally speaking, we can't see very far into the future but God reveals as He leads and it is only as we look back that we see how He has prepared us beforehand for the different situations we encounter in our lives.

As I write, I think again of the way God has worked in my own life and, especially, the spiritual 'springtimes' I have experienced over the years as I have been willing to commit myself to go adventuring with Him.

Soon after the first weekend, I received a lovely card from 'Margaret' who writes: 'Although I am in "winter" I see it now as a time of Sabbath – rest and new growth rather than a dead and dark season in my life. Following the death of my husband last year, in several things at church, the doors seemed to close on me and I felt a guilt as though I was being disobedient not wanting to continue with these duties. But when Beth said, "Winter is a time of preparation for new growth" (ie the bulbs), I realised God is allowing me this time of rest and I am looking forward to Him opening new doors for me, but in His time, not mine.'

We are praying, dear reader, that God will use the things that we have shared in this book to bless and prepare you and draw you close to Himself. Whether this is a time when you are 'adventuring with God' and embarking on an exciting new phase in your life, a spiritual spring or a season of rest and waiting, may you experience the reality of God at work in your life in a powerful way.

Jeannette and Beverley
March 2004

Chapter One

Seasonal Living

Beverley Shepherd

'There is a time for everything, and a season for every activity under heaven ...'

(Ecclesiastes 3:1)

When God created the world He gave us seasons – a pattern of living where each season has a different pace and focus.

> There is a time for everything,
> and a season for every activity under heaven:
> a time to be born and a time to die,
> a time to plant and a time to uproot,
> a time to kill and a time to heal
> What does the worker gain from his toil? I have seen the burden God has laid on men. He has made everything beautiful in its time. He has also set eternity in the hearts of men; yet they cannot fathom what God has done from beginning to end.
>
> (Eccl. 3:1–11)

Some seasons are filled with activity and others are times of preparation or of rest. Learning to live in harmony with the seasons of our life is vital if we are to work with God in this world. Misjudging the season can leave us tired and frustrated.

Seasonal living is not about our age or even the time of year – it is about learning to discern God's rhythms and patterns and then aligning ourselves with Him so that we move at His pace. These patterns can be weekly, monthly, yearly, seven-yearly or over a lifetime.

In the Old Testament God gave Israel some patterns they were to observe as a nation:

▦ The Sabbath day: 'Six days you shall labour and do all your work, but the seventh day is a Sabbath to the LORD your God' (Exod. 20:9–10).

▦ The Sabbath year: 'For six years you are to sow your fields and harvest the crops, but during the seventh year let the land lie unploughed and unused' (Exod. 23:10–11).

▓ The Jubilee year: 'The fiftieth year shall be a jubilee for you; do
   not sow and do not reap what grows of itself or harvest the
   untended vines. For it is a jubilee and is to be holy for you' (Lev.
   25:11–12).

As well as the Sabbath patterns there were regular feasts and
festivals to be observed: the Passover, Harvest and Firstfruits, Weeks,
Trumpets, the Day of Atonement, Tabernacles. These all added a
rhythm to the life of the community.

We live in a day and age where seasonal living is much harder and
yet more necessary. For many of us the only speed we know is 'full
ahead'. We no longer know how to stop because we believe the lie that
there isn't enough time. Stopping is a luxury we cannot afford. In the
midst of this frenetic busyness we are expected to lead 'balanced' lives.
The 'Superwoman' role model encourages us to have an exciting
career, bring up a family, have a perfect house, go to the gym three
times a week, take up some creative hobby and still find 'quality' time
to spend with husband, children and God! No wonder we are
exhausted or haunted by a sense of failure!

Increasingly this world's music forces us to maximise the use of
every moment, multitask at every opportunity – make that call on
your mobile while driving, read that article while eating and give time
to your spouse while watching TV. Our lives have stopped making
sense. Like a long paragraph with all the punctuation and spaces
between words taken out, our lives fail to convey any meaning.

We humans have chosen speed and we thrive on it – more than
we generally admit. Our ability to work fast and play fast gives us
power. It thrills us. If we have learned the name of just one
hormone, it is adrenaline. 'Time is a gentle deity,' said Sophocles.

Perhaps it was, for him. Today it cracks the whip. [1]

Our dream is to be faster than the next person, so we speed up, and so do they, and the world gets faster. We pick up each other's rhythms and the accumulated rhythms of the world around us. If most of the rhythms around us are fast, so are ours, automatically. 'Balance' is a myth, and not a concept advocated in the Bible. Instead the Bible talks of seasons – of a pace that varies between busyness and rest.

It is into the context of our frenetic lifestyles that Jesus speaks and offers a different way of living:

'Are you tired? Worn out? Burned out on religion? Come to me. Get away with me and you'll recover your life. I'll show you how to take a real rest. Walk with me and work with me – watch how I do it. Learn the unforced rhythms of grace. I won't lay anything heavy or ill-fitting on you. Keep company with me and you'll learn to live freely and lightly.'

(Matt. 11:28–30, *The Message*)

The seasons of the year are a helpful framework for thinking about seasonal living and in which to learn 'the unforced rhythms of grace'.

Winter

Winter is the season of rest. Not rest in terms of putting your feet up, but in terms of Sabbath rest. It is a time of refocusing on who God is and celebrating His love for us and all He has done for us – a time of putting our roots deep down into God and experiencing His renewal. To live in winter, and in order to avoid the busyness of previous seasons, we have to learn to say 'No'. In doing this we may have to confront our addiction to activity and realise that our worth is not based on what we do, but on who we are in Christ.

Winter is the starting point. God calls us to 'work from rest' and not 'rest from work'. Unless we have effectively 'wintered' we cannot hope for growth in spring and fruitfulness in summer.

Spring

I love the spring in England – the first snowdrops and crocuses, followed by hosts of daffodils and colourful tulips. The air is still crisp but the sun is bright. Spring is a season of new growth – exploring new areas and watching God do a 'new thing' in our lives. It can be an exciting time with a tremendous sense of expansion and new horizons. It is as if God is opening the doors and we are free to walk through them with energy and anticipation. Like Joshua on the verge of the promised land, God's word to us is 'Have I not commanded you? Be strong and courageous. Do not be terrified; do not be discouraged, for the LORD your God will be with you wherever you go' (Josh. 1:9). Notice that even after 40 years of preparation in the desert as Moses' assistant, Joshua is terrified. It's not wrong to be nervous as new doors open – it can be our fear that encourages us to lean more fully on God and His resources, rather than trusting in our own abilities.

Summer

The abundant growth of spring should result in fruit – 'You did not choose me, but I chose you and appointed you to go and bear fruit – fruit that will last' (John 15:16). Summer is the time when we fulfil our calling to be fruit-bearers; a time where the deep work of God in our lives is evidenced. Christians are meant to be known by their fruit. It can also be a time of danger: we see the fruit and think it is the result of our own skill and work.

You may say to yourself, 'My power and the strength of my hands have produced this wealth for me.' But remember the Lord your God, for it is he who gives you the ability to produce wealth, and so confirms his covenant, which he swore to your forefathers, as it is today. (Deut. 8:17–18)

The fruit of summer is not the result of our own striving – it results from abiding, being firmly rooted in God and obedient to His commands. The fruit is the result of the preparation of winter and the growth of spring. It is designed to be a blessing to both ourselves and others.

Autumn

Autumn is the season where we 'bottle the fruit' and prepare to be pruned back. Bottling the fruit is about 'ending well', ensuring that we have completed all that is necessary before we either close an activity down or hand it on. Ending well requires discipline and perseverance, and rarely carries with it the excitement we experienced at the start of a project or role. There can be a sense of loss, and this will be particularly great where our identity has been linked with a project or activity. Also, we may experience the temptation to focus on potential new beginnings rather than bringing things to a rightful close.

Joshua was someone who ended well. In Joshua 24:31 we read, 'Israel served the Lord throughout the lifetime of Joshua and of the elders who outlived him and who had experienced everything the Lord had done for Israel.'

Joshua's whole life is an example of seasonal living. He was prepared during the 40 years in the desert (winter), grew as he led the Israelites into the promised land (spring), gradually conquered the land and allocated it to the different tribes (summer), and finally led all the tribes of Israel to renew their covenant commitment to God at

Shechem – a sealing of all that had been achieved (autumn); before entering his final rest and being buried in the promised land.

Living out-of-season can lead us away from God's best for us, and may result in sin. There is evidence of this in the lives of David and Martha. In the lives of Mary, Esther and Jesus we can see the power of living in tune with God's timing.

David

The story of David's adultery with Bathsheba is told in 2 Samuel 11 and begins like this: 'In the spring, at the time when kings go off to war, David sent Joab out with the king's men and the whole Israelite army. They destroyed the Ammonites and besieged Rabbah. But David remained in Jerusalem' (v.1).

There was a season for war and spring was it! The ground was firm so that the army could march easily and the wheels of the chariots would not get bogged down. Summer would be too hot and in autumn the men were needed to gather in the harvest. That spring, David's rightful place was at the head of his army and yet we find him in Jerusalem, walking around on the roof of the palace, with time on his hands. It is there that he sees Bathsheba, and adultery and murder follow. It is not only Uriah, Bathsheba's husband that is murdered, but also those soldiers that are left stranded with him – many families were affected by David's decision to stay in Jerusalem when it was spring.

Esther

'Before a girl's turn came to go in to King Xerxes, she had to complete twelve months of beauty treatments prescribed for the women, six months with oil of myrrh and six with perfumes and cosmetics.' (Esth. 2:12)

'And who knows but that you have come to royal position for such a time as this?' (Esth. 4:14)

Before Esther goes in to the king she has a year to prepare – a year when she is hidden away, not even revealing her nationality or family. It is a year with one focus – to be chosen as queen. Esther takes her preparation seriously – taking advice from Hegai, the king's eunuch who was in charge of the harem. There is no sense in the text, that Esther is impatient for her turn to visit the king – she stays willingly in the season of preparation until the right time comes. Then she goes in to the king, wins his favour and is made queen. Throughout this, God's purposes are being worked out. It is Mordecai, her uncle, who discerns that her royal office is not a matter of chance but of divine providence. When Haman, the prime minister, issues an edict in the king's name, that all the Jews are to be slaughtered, Esther comes to recognise that her preparation and role are for 'such a time as this' and is used by God to deliver the Jewish people. Mordecai makes it clear that although deliverance does not depend on Esther, missing out on her appointed time will have dire consequences for her: 'For if you remain silent at this time, relief and deliverance for the Jews will arise from another place, but you and your father's family will perish' (Esth. 4:14).

Martha and Mary

'Martha, Martha,' the Lord answered, 'you are worried and upset about many things, but only one thing is needed. Mary has chosen what is better, and it will not be taken away from her.'

(Luke 10: 41–42)

The story of Martha and Mary has often perplexed me. Is Jesus commending the listening of Mary over the activity of Martha in every situation? Is there never a role for 'doing' as well as listening? Or is it that Martha has misjudged the season? Will this be one of the last opportunities to sit and listen to Jesus before His death – the last chance for Him to say important things to these two sisters whom He loved?

I suspect that Martha was someone who liked to be prepared and have everything 'just so' when guests arrived, and part of Middle Eastern hospitality is to offer a meal to guests in your home. Perhaps one of the reasons that Jesus has enjoyed their home so much is the sense of welcome that such preparation can give. And yet Jesus is quite clear that, on this occasion, Mary has chosen what is better. It is Mary who has understood the timing of this visit and recognised that 'only one thing is needed'. Martha presumes on what is needed rather than listening to Jesus and, through her distraction, misses out. Mary, staying close to Jesus and listening to Him, recognises what is important.

Jesus

'My time has not yet come.' (John 2:4)
'Father, the time has come. Glorify your Son, that your Son may glorify you.' (John 17:1)
'It is finished.' (John 19:30)

Throughout His life Jesus shows great awareness of His Father's timing. He responds to this timing and is able to say, on the cross, 'It is finished.'

From these few examples we can see that discerning God's timing and seasons in our lives is important. There are two Greek words for time – *kairos* and *chronos*. *Kairos* carries with it the sense of an appointed time, the right time, the opportunity for some event or action that advances God's purposes; whereas *chronos* refers to the passing of time – the minutes, hours and days. My hope for all of us is that we increasingly use our days and hours, our *chronos* time, to serve God's purposes, His *kairos*.

Discerning our season

How then are we to know which season we are in? Like Mary we have to learn to listen: listen to God, to our circumstances, to our bodies and to wise counsellors.

Listening to God

God wants us to align ourselves with His seasons in our lives and so, when we are willing to listen to Him on this, we can expect that He will show us. He may use our reading of the Bible, prayer or even, as in my own case, a dream (I will explain this more fully at the end of the chapter).

Listening to our circumstances

For some people there is a natural flow of seasons in the structure of their lives, for example, farmers whose year is geared around the weather, or teachers with the school year pattern of terms and holidays. For others there may be particular circumstances that lead us into a season such as illness. I am a trainer and remember one year when there were two consecutive months without work – there was plenty of work booked for the months following on from this period, but whenever I tried to book training for these two months my clients either wanted it on a later date or cancelled! Eventually I 'got the message' and asked God to show me His agenda for this two-month period!

Listening to our bodies

God has designed us to get tired! After a period of busyness and activity, or of personal trauma or loss, it is appropriate to feel tired and in need of a quieter season in which to allow God's deep work of restoration and renewal to take place. Sometimes we have caused our own tiredness by taking on uncommanded work or by being unwise in the hours we keep, and it is here that we may need a trusted friend to confront us.

Listening to a wise counsellor

I have the privilege of having a prayer partner with whom I meet every four to six weeks for a Saturday morning. We catch up on each other's lives and then pray with and for each other – seeking to discern God's hand in each other's circumstances. Part of God's gift to us is that we always seem to be in opposite seasons and hence what God is speaking into each of our lives at any one time is very different. Sometimes He has used one of us to confront the other with over-busyness and sometimes to encourage the other to move, with God, into the next season.

The dream

When God first started to speak to me about seasonal living He used a dream to get my attention. We all dream – or so I'm told – it's just that I don't normally remember mine. So when, in August 1999, I awoke with every detail of a dream vividly etched on my memory, I knew God had spoken.

The dream concerned a rail journey. I was travelling by train to a large city, arriving at one terminus and then needing to continue my journey from a second terminus some way across the city. Bicycles were provided to cross the city, but I only had three minutes to make my connection. I pedalled furiously whilst clutching a parcel containing something very precious. Worn out, I arrived at the second terminus with time to spare, but had lost the parcel! Still, with my thirty remaining seconds I could retrace my journey and find it – or so I thought. The precious parcel had disappeared and in its place I collected several other parcels – all jiffy bags full of bubble wrap.

I dashed back to the second terminus and leapt onto the train as it was pulling out of the station. Making my way to a corner seat I collapsed, absolutely exhausted, and surrounded by my parcels full of nothing. It was then that I awoke.

I knew the dream had been a warning – 'What was in that first parcel that was so precious?' was my anxious question as I prayed. God showed me. I picked up my diary and started to rearrange my schedule. My diary is not that easy to reorganise, with many events being booked several months in advance. Six months later the changes started to bear fruit and I realised with both shock and gratitude that God's warning had come just in time.

The changes I made to my diary reflected the principles of 'working from rest' – of building into my life weekly, monthly and yearly patterns and starting each of these cycles with times of drawing aside to listen to God. That listening involves discerning His priorities and perspective on the work and relationships I am called to, but first and foremost it is the time when I remember who I am – His beloved daughter in whom He is well pleased. Everything flows from this understanding.

What might you lose if you continue to live at your current pace – your laughter and spontaneity, your sense of fun, your peace, your vision, your most cherished relationships? Only you know what is at stake, and only you can choose to change.

Jeannette and I invite you to journey with us as we explore the seasons together and our prayer is that you discover the 'unforced rhythms of grace'.

Questions for reflection

■ Have you been aware of 'seasons' in your life?

■ What season are you currently in?

– What is God saying?

– What are your circumstances saying?

– What is your body saying?

– What are trusted friends saying?

■ How might you give yourself more fully to the season you are in?

■ What are you in danger of losing if you carry on at a frenetic pace?

Notes
1. *Faster*, James Gleick (Little, Brown & Co., 1999).

Chapter Two

Winter

Beverley Shepherd

Original sessions given by Beth Clark

'Be still, and know that I am God'

(Psa. 46:10)

Winter can be a season we dread. Our feelings are summed up in the hymn: 'In the bleak mid winter, frosty wind made moan' and we shiver with the thought of the cold. In *The Lion, the Witch and the Wardrobe*, by C.S. Lewis, the children enter the kingdom ruled by the Ice Queen and are told that here it is forever winter, but never Christmas. For us it is different – when God draws us into winter He promises us Christmas, Emmanuel, God with us. Winter is our opportunity to meet with God in a deep and intimate way; a time when we can draw close to Him. It is a time to rest, refocus and put our roots deep down into God. The focus is on the activity below the ground, not above it.

In one of my gardening books, *The Weekend Gardener*, by Monty Don,[1] there is a weather report for January:

> There is no avoiding it, this is winter. January is either cold and wet or just freezing. This does the garden no harm and potentially quite a lot of good, because a bout of really cold weather will kill off a lot of the bugs and diseases and stop the land getting too waterlogged. A spell of unseasonably mild weather is more worrying, as plants will think it is spring, start to grow and then be cruelly cut back by the inevitable cold spell that will come along before spring proper.

Monty Don goes on to say that this is a good time to:

- walk around the garden, taking stock of the layout and design
- get your gardening equipment sharpened and serviced
- buy inspiring gardening books and plan for the year ahead.

I believe we can learn much from this gardening analogy. In winter God gives us the opportunity to rest, take stock, plan ahead and prepare. He also uses it to kill off the bugs of pride and impatience that flourish in the busy months. Our danger, like that of the garden, is that we will stay too warm, or active, and not fully obey God's command to 'Be still, and know that I am God' (Psa. 46:10).

Let us examine several key features of winter: stopping, resting, killing the bugs, refocusing and preparation.

Stopping

In a busy world like ours how do we stop? Firstly, we have to want to; stopping is most effective when it is a choice. A few years ago I was due to co-lead a mission team with a well-known evangelist. He was an incredibly busy man, and eventually had to pull out due to illness. The comment of his secretary was enlightening: 'Illness is God's way of stopping him, otherwise he would be on the go the whole time.' If we don't choose to stop, then we may be forced to at some stage, but forced stops rarely contain the peace and restorative value of a planned stop.

Often we don't stop because we believe that time is scarce. If we are to challenge and dethrone the belief that there isn't enough time, we have to take a good look at the character of God the Creator. God is a God of abundance – we see it all around us. Millions of seeds, but only a few may be germinated. Millions of stars, but only one may be inhabited. Five thousand fed, and twelve baskets left over. Is it possible that this abundantly generous God could be stingy in one area of His creation – time? That He would have deliberately withheld those much needed extra two hours a day that we need to get everything done? That he should have prepared in advance good works for us to do (Eph. 2:10) and yet not given us enough time to do them? No! God has given us more than enough time – even time to waste! Let's believe it and know that there is enough time to stop.

When, as a result of the dream mentioned in the previous chapter, I started to stop, I was faced with the question: 'Who am I when I stop?' Very often our identity can get linked to our activity and we don't feel of worth if we are not doing something. Stopping both confronts issues of identity and yet also provides us with the opportunity to centre our identity more fully in Christ.

In his book *Stopping*, David Kundtz indicates three ways to stop[2]:

- *Still points*: those moments during the day that are given to us to think or reflect, eg waiting at red traffic lights, the supermarket queue, the meeting that doesn't start on time etc. Too often we miss them, or waste them by being impatient for them to end.

- *Stop-overs*: these are longer periods of time, perhaps an afternoon, a weekend, a quiet day where we deliberately give ourselves some space in which to reflect and slow the pace. This year I have started going to a Christian retreat house for a day a month, with no agenda except to be with God, to pray, read my Bible and reflect on what God is saying. These stopovers help me refocus for the month ahead.

- *Grinding halts*: I don't like the term grinding halt because it infers a forced stop, yet the reality is that if we do not plan to have winter seasons then we may well be brought to a grinding halt.

I don't know what 'stopping' will look like in your life – that is something for you and God to work out together. It will, however, be a season where time is made to have hours alone with God and activity will be cut back to a minimum.

Resting

When God created the world He made man on the sixth day and commissioned man and woman to work in the garden (Gen. 2:15). On the seventh day God rested, so man and woman's first full day was a day of rest! Rest is always the starting point of our walk with God. Sunday is the first day of the week – a time for restoration, for rediscovering who we are in God, and focusing on His priorities for the next six days.

Rest is one of the great promises of the Bible. In Matthew 11:28–30 the familiar words of Jesus reiterate this promise:

'Come to me, all you who are weary and burdened, and I will give you rest. Take my yoke upon you and learn from me, for I am gentle and humble in heart, and you will find rest for your souls. For my yoke is easy and my burden is light.'

Notice that rest is a gift – a gift that is dependent on coming to Jesus. It is not collapsing in a heap at the end of an exhausting day – instead there is a sense of a burden being shouldered by someone else; Jesus is taking charge and carrying the responsibility.

One of my great heroes is Hudson Taylor. A pioneer missionary to inland China, he established the China Inland Mission (now OMF) and carried huge responsibility for the operation of the mission and the welfare of the missionaries. Those that met him were struck by how untroubled and peaceful he was. His secret: true rest. In a letter to his sister he describes his experience of rest:

The sweetest part, if one may speak of one part being sweeter than another, is the rest which full identification with Christ brings. I am no longer anxious about anything, as I realise this: for He, I know, is able to carry out His will, and His will is mine. It makes no matter where He places me, or how. That is rather for Him to consider than for me; for in the easiest position He must give me His grace, and in the most difficult His grace is sufficient.[3]

I believe true rest is only possible if we believe that, as the psalmist puts it,

One thing God has spoken,
    two things have I heard:
that you, O God, are strong,
    and that you, O Lord, are loving. (Psa. 62:11–12)

It is the deep-seated belief that God is strong (able to do all that He promises) and loving (committed to my salvation and blessing; committed to working things together for good) that gives me the security to rest. I can rest in the passenger seat, knowing that His hands are on the steering wheel and that He has planned the route.

Killing the bugs

It is when we stop that we are confronted with our own pride and impatience, because we have no choice but to be dependent on God and wait. In the desert the Israelites couldn't cultivate their own food and so they needed God to provide manna. Each day (except the Sabbath) they went out to collect enough for that day. They weren't allowed to store it overnight as it would go mouldy – they had to trust that God would provide again tomorrow. Such dependency can feel scary to us – we prefer to think that we are in control. Yet even when we earn a wage or salary, we are not in control – God is still the ultimate provider.

Eighteen years ago I was made redundant. I walked into the office one day at 9 am and had left by 9.30 am. I was given one month's salary in lieu of notice, told to clear my desk, and bring back the keys to the car at the end of the month! I was catapulted into winter! God indicated that I was not to get a job in the same industry but to wait until He showed me the next step. I can write this quite calmly now, having seen how wonderfully God provided, but at the time it was scary. I was out of control and totally dependent on His provision to pay the mortgage and food bills. It was a time of miracles – cheques arrived through the post, overpaid tax was refunded and I learned to economise. The bug of pride was frozen out by the gratitude I felt for God's generous provision.

Because winter is a time of waiting we are faced with our impatience. We live in an instant world. One of the first credit cards came with the slogan 'It takes the waiting out of wanting' and we have come to believe that waiting is a bad thing. In the Bible, waiting contains the promise 'they who wait for the LORD shall renew their strength' (Isa. 40:31, NRSV). Waiting is not empty, but a time of preparation, as in pregnancy. Just as the baby awaits its appointed time to be born, so our waiting depends on God's appointed time for leading us into the next season. If a baby is born prematurely, then it is not fully formed. Similarly, if we cut short our waiting, then whatever God is birthing in us will be undeveloped. Let the waiting of winter kill the bug of impatience in us.

Refocusing

In winter there is the time to refocus on what is important, not just in terms of activity, but more significantly through a reshaping of our identity. In the busy seasons of life we are encouraged in Western society to draw our identity from our activity. In winter God reminds us that we are first and foremost His beloved children:

> For you did not receive a spirit that makes you a slave again to fear, but you received the Spirit of sonship. And by him we cry, '*Abba*, Father.' The Spirit himself testifies with our spirit that we are God's children.' (Rom. 8:15–16)

The knowledge that we are adopted as God's children through Christ's death and resurrection frees us from having to earn our acceptance through achievement and activity. We start from a place of acceptance, belonging and security! As we sustain our relationship with God through worship, prayer, Bible reading and fellowship we become secure in the knowledge of His love for us – our true identity. If we fail to draw our identity from our relationship with God we can develop an orphan spirit: 'But for those like us, our fate is to face the world as orphans, chasing through long years the shadows of vanished parents. There is nothing for it but to try and see through our missions to the end, as best we can, for until we do so, we will be permitted no calm.' That is how Christopher Banks, hero of *When we were Orphans*,[4] summarised his life.

The orphan spirit is a spirit of drivenness, the attempt to justify our existence and prove our acceptablility through achievement and activity. It leads to the unending search for belonging and approval – unending because no achievement or amount of activity can fully satisfy our need for acceptance – there is no getting off the treadmill.

When secure in our identity in God, we are free to do the work He leads us into, and refuse the work that is not ours. In Mark 1:35–38, Jesus, having spent time with His Father, has a clarity of purpose that enables Him to stand against the many claims upon Him and respond to the most important claim – that of God's purpose in His life.

Very early in the morning, while it was still dark, Jesus got up, left the house and went off to a solitary place, where he prayed. Simon and his companions went to look for him, and when they found him, they exclaimed: 'Everyone is looking for you!' Jesus replied, 'Let us go somewhere else – to the nearby villages – so that I can preach there also. That is why I have come.'

God has work that He has prepared for each one of us (Eph. 2:10) and He will reveal His purposes in our lives as we give time to listening to Him, as Mary did, rather than being a distracted Martha. Beware the danger of thinking that this 'work' is some great achievement or activity – often it is the 'small' things that are God's work for us that day: the comforting word to someone who is hurting, the encouraging of a child to read, tea and chat with a lonely neighbour or doing diligently and faithfully the work for which we are employed.

The 'prayer of examen' is the spiritual discipline of reviewing the day at its close, and asking for God's wisdom to discern the works that were within His purpose, and those that we allowed to distract us. Through this we can grow in wisdom and become more responsive to His leading. The good news is that there is forgiveness for when we get it wrong, as we will!

Preparing

'Enlarge the place of your tent, stretch your tent curtains wide, do not hold back; lengthen your cords, strengthen your stakes. For you will spread out to the right and to the left …' (Isa. 54:2–3)

God calls us to prepare for the work He wants to do in us and through us. Winter is the time to prepare, but we do so in the sure and certain knowledge that spring and summer will follow – that we will spread out to the right and to the left.

How then do we prepare, especially if the full picture of what God is calling us into is not clear? We 'enlarge the place of our tent' by making space in our lives for the new thing that God wants to do, and we 'strengthen our stakes' by becoming more firmly anchored in God through deepened faith.

Making space in our lives is similar to clearing the leaves and pruning back the shrubs in the garden – clearing out the old in order to make way for new growth. This may involve very practical things like clearing out cupboards, tidying our financial affairs and getting fit. It could also involve pruning back activities or certain relationships. Some friends of mine were led into a winter period, not knowing what the new thing was that God had for them. They decided to clear out the attic and garage, getting rid of paper work from years before and giving away items they no longer needed. When the opportunity opened up suddenly for them to join the staff of a church in Australia – halfway across the world, their house was immediately ready to be put on the market!

Strengthening our stakes: when Hudson Taylor was called by God to go to China, he knew that he would need to prepare. This preparation involved learning Chinese and studying medicine, yet he was aware that he also needed to prepare spiritually. He wrote: 'When I get out to China I shall have no claim on anyone for anything. My only claim will be on God. How important to learn, before leaving England, to move man, through God, by prayer alone.'[5] He used his existing circumstances to practise exercising faith, taking matters of concern to God in prayer and mentioning them to no one else. As he experienced God's faithfulness, his 'faith muscles' grew.

Very often, the comfort of our lifestyles means that our faith muscles have grown flabby. When I was made redundant I would pray before I went shopping that God would direct me to the right shop to find the things I needed at the lowest price. I can still remember the joy with which I returned home, having received abundantly more than I had asked for! Since my bank balance has become 'healthier', shopping does not carry the same level of excitement, or the need to exercise faith in the same way.

If we are to get spiritually fit, then we need to ask God for appropriate ways in which to exercise and grow our faith.

The season of winter is God's gift to us, a time to regain our bearings and develop a greater intimacy with God. Spring and summer will follow, but we will only be able to make the most of their opportunities if we have allowed God to quiet us with His love and strengthen our faith.

Questions for reflection

■ What was your last experience of 'winter'?

■ What did you enjoy about it?

■ What did you find difficult?

■ What prevents you 'stopping' for stopovers or for longer periods?

■ How is God currently asking you to prepare?

Notes

1. *The Weekend Gardener* by Monty Don (Bloomsbury, 1997).
2. *Stopping* by David Kundtz (Newleaf, 1998).
3. *Hudson Taylor's Spiritual Secret* by Dr and Mrs Howard Taylor (Discovery House, 1990).
4. *When We Were Orphans* by Kazuo Ishiguro (Faber and Faber, 2000).
5. *Hudson Taylor's Spiritual Secret*, op. cit.

Chapter Three

Spring

Jeannette Barwick

'See! The winter is past;
the rains are over and gone.
Flowers appear on the earth;
the season of singing has come,
the cooing of doves
is heard in our land.'

(Songs 2:11–12)

Who does not love the spring after the long, dark days of winter? In different ways in different lands nature proclaims the season, yet unmistakably conveys a clear message of new life, new birth and new growth. Springtime in the northern hemisphere also embraces the Easter celebration with its message of resurrection life and the ultimate gift of eternal life.

Having grown strong through our winter experiences we can look beyond them to the new life and promise of the spring when the Lord will say to us:

'See! The winter is past;
    the rains are over and gone.
Flowers appear on the earth;
    the season of singing has come,
the cooing of doves
    is heard in our land.
The fig-tree forms its early fruit;
    the blossoming vines spread their fragrance.
Arise, come, my darling;
    my beautiful one, come with me.' (Songs 2:11–13)

Spring is an exciting time spiritually, too, and full of promise. We may not be able to see very far ahead in the way the Lord is leading us but we can sense the excitement of the call in our spirit. As a plant begins to grow, its potential is there but its final form is as yet unrevealed. So too for us: while we see only the early signs of new growth, God sees the final flowering, but only gradually reveals His purposes.

Let me now tell you about a spiritual 'spring' in my life, over 25 years ago. My young daughters were both in school and I found myself with time and enthusiasm for other things! Very soon God showed me that He wanted me to begin something at our church, for mothers with young children from the local community. For me the word 'something' has huge spiritual significance. I did not know, initially, what that 'something' was to be, but at the same time God spoke also to my friend, quite separately. We got together to pray and discuss possibilities, talked to other friends and then approached our minister. The idea that emerged was to create a welcoming place for young mothers where they and their children could meet and make friends. We also wanted to share our love relationship with Jesus with them through our friendship. How it would all unfold we did not know but our minister was most encouraging, saying: 'Just begin and see where it all leads.'

With his blessing we named our project 'OASIS – refreshment in a barren suburban desert', had some cards printed and left them in the baby clinic and doctors' surgeries. We met for the first time as the OASIS Mother and Toddlers Group on a Tuesday morning, in the small hall at the rear of our church and, to my recollection, about 16 mothers and children came. We were off! We could not, of course, foresee how things would progress but after each meeting we had lunch together and prayed, and God faithfully showed us the next steps.

OASIS grew at an amazing rate, and we then began monthly outreach meetings with speakers who gave powerful testimony. Some gave their lives to Christ and we began monthly Bible study and prayer groups. Health visitors and social workers would bring 'special case' needy mums to us, such as single parents in their teens, and often, I will confess, we felt out of our depth as we encountered women with huge problems in their lives. The care professionals said to us, 'We don't know how you care for them individually in such a large group, but you do.' To our great encouragement, they brought women in from other areas to see what we were doing so that similar groups could be established in the surrounding district.

Why am I telling you all this? Because God was doing a new thing in our midst: giving us a spiritual 'spring'. We were not 'special people' in any way, but God was at work and, as we prayed and cried out to Him in situation after situation, He was faithful. He enabled us, for instance, to come alongside the young mother whose beautiful little boy died a cot death, and the heavily pregnant mother abandoned with her first child less than a year old. He worked miracles of healing and finance and accommodation. There were marriages in jeopardy: some were saved and are sound and strong today, others could not be saved, but all of us were drawn more deeply into life with Christ. God guided us each step of the way and we gave Him the praise and thanks for all that He brought about during those years. For me, the things I learnt during those eight years were the foundation of much that He has led me into since.

Adventuring with God

Our spiritual 'springs' are times of adventure with God, times of responding fully to His prompting and direction, not of pursuing our own ideas, keeping Him in the background or simply asking for His rubber stamp of approval. Adventuring with God may mean moving into new territory and this can be exciting and challenging, but it may also cause us to feel fearful and apprehensive.

This was exactly how I felt 20 years ago when, not long after my joining CWR, at that time located conveniently near to my home, it was decided to open a Counselling Centre in the next town, Walton on Thames, and I was asked to move there to set it up and run it. I was reluctant to do this, for, being a sociable person, I loved being part of a team and working at the new Centre would mean spending a great deal of time on my own. After viewing the new premises, I asked the Lord, 'Do you really want me to do this? I don't want to leave the others and work alone. Please show me.' In my Bible reading that very night I read: 'I sat alone because your hand was on me' (Jer. 15:17), and I knew at once that God was guiding me to take up this challenge. The two or so years I spent in Walton were, I realised afterwards, a time of transition for me before I began working even further away from home, in roles that would eventually take me to many different countries.

The next move was in 1987, to become a member of a small team based at Waverley Abbey House, the new headquarters of the CWR ministry founded by Selwyn Hughes. Driving back to the Counselling Centre from viewing Waverley Abbey House with Selwyn just before its official opening in 1987, I exclaimed, 'How I would love to begin "something" for women in that beautiful place!' What was it to be? I did not know then but, about six months into the programme at Waverley Abbey House, I made a request to the Directors to begin outreach meetings for women. The outcome has been a Bible-based teaching ministry to women that has now been established at Waverley for over a decade and a half. Through day and weekend events and publications especially for women, it has reached thousands of women on four continents. It is amazing to see what has been accomplished with God's enabling.

So, my message to you is that we all need to respond to the opportunities God provides even though we don't have clear sight of the way ahead. Our whole future is not mapped out before us and we might be overwhelmed if we knew 'up front' everything God has planned. We simply need to be obedient and begin with the things we know He wants us to do. God will be faithful to reveal His purposes more specifically along the way.

Sometimes, as was the case for Joshua, the call to new activity means involvement as leaders in a new phase of an existing ministry. The book of Joshua is a book of encouragement for us today: leaders don't lead forever. There comes a time in every ministry when God calls for a new beginning with a new generation and new leadership. Except for Joshua and Caleb, the old generation of Israelites had perished during the nation's wanderings in the wilderness; and Moses commissioned Joshua to lead the new generation into a new challenge: entering and conquering the promised land. 'God buries His workmen,' it is said, 'but His work goes on.' It was God who had chosen Joshua, and everybody in Israel recognised him as their new leader.

A wise leader doesn't completely abandon the past but builds on it as he or she moves towards the future. Moses is mentioned 57 times in the book of Joshua, evidence that Joshua respected Moses and what he had done for Israel. Joshua and Moses worshipped the same God and obeyed the same word that God gave through Moses to the nation. There was continuity from one leader to the next, but there wasn't conformity, for each leader is unique and must maintain his or her individuality. Joshua, like Moses, was called the servant of God (Josh. 24:29) and what is important is not the servant but the Master.

In the calling and commissioning of Joshua (Josh. 1:1–18), God gave him two promises: first, that he would possess the land of Canaan and, second, that God would be with him and would never forsake him.

The Lord directs him to the secret of success – meditation on the Word of God: 'Do not let this Book of the Law depart from your mouth; meditate on it day and night, so that you may be careful to do everything written in it. Then you will be prosperous and successful' (Josh. 1:8).

It is this more than any other single thing that made Joshua the great leader he proved to be.

Doubtless you know how to read the Bible, study the Bible and even memorise the Bible – but let me ask you, do you know how to *meditate* on it? Research shows that only one in ten thousand Christians understands and practises the principles of meditation. The words used in the Hebrew for meditation – *hagah* and *siyach* – mean to ponder, imagine, contemplate, reflect, pray, commune, murmur, mutter and converse with oneself. In other words, meditation means to roll a word, thought or phrase around in the mind, continually contemplating, pondering and dwelling upon it, viewing it from every angle, weighing it and considering it carefully. We need to do this, not just once, but over and over again, until we begin to talk to ourselves about it and allow it to penetrate, permeate and saturate our thinking.[1]

Scripture meditation, then, is the digestive process of the soul, of vital importance to spiritual development. It is the process whereby we absorb, internalise and apply truth in our daily lives so that we can grow and work for God's kingdom.[2]

Like Joshua, we can be enabled by God's grace to take charge of our circumstances and, as we follow God's command to meditate on His Word day and night, we are empowered not only to believe but also to enter into His promise.

What stops us moving forward with God?

A faulty concept of God

How do you see God? Are you perhaps like the young woman who, in counselling, described God in the same way she described her father: 'Distant, cold, uncommunicative.' Women often transfer memories of their own fathers onto God, seeing Him as uncaring or untrustworthy, rather than as a good and loving Father in whom we can have full confidence.

But, in truth, He is love – *all* love (1 John 4:16). If you took everything else away, love would be left. In C.S. Lewis's book, *The Lion, the Witch and the Wardrobe*, the Lion, Aslan, stands, in a sense, for the figure of Christ, and there comes a moment when the children hear Aslan roaring in the distance:

'Is – is he a man?' asked Lucy. 'Is Aslan a man!' said Mr Beaver sternly. 'Certainly not. I tell you he is the King of the wood and the Son of the great Emperor-beyond-the-sea. Don't you know who is King of Beasts? Aslan is a lion – *the* Lion, the great Lion'. 'Ooh!' said Susan, 'I thought he was a man. Is he – quite safe? I shall feel rather nervous about meeting a lion.' 'That you will, dear, and no mistake,' said Mrs Beaver; 'if there's anyone who can appear before Aslan without their knees knocking, they're either braver than most or else just silly.' 'Then he isn't safe?' said Lucy. 'Safe?' said Mr Beaver; 'don't you hear what Mrs Beaver tells you? Who said anything about safe? Course he isn't safe. But he's good.'[5]

In the goodness of God we can have confidence. The challenge is whether we can trust Him when we cannot trace Him? It's difficult for us to move forward and adventure with God if we have a faulty concept of Him. You will never reach higher in your Christian life, it has been said, than your concept of God. The way you see Him will determine the way you worship Him, work for Him and witness to Him.

A faulty concept of yourself

How we see God determines how we see ourselves: if we have a wrong concept of God, we will have a wrong concept of ourselves and so many women I speak to suffer with low self-esteem. Do you believe that, when God made you, He made you right? One of the most wonderful scriptures, to my mind, is Ephesians 2:10 (NKJV): 'For we are His workmanship, created in Christ Jesus for good works, which God prepared beforehand that we should walk in them.' This means that *you* are God's workmanship and when He made you, He did well because He cannot do otherwise.

Rid yourself right now of any thoughts you might have that you are not worthy: you are of great worth because the Son of God died for you. Believe that when God made you He made you right. I don't, of course, mean that you're perfect now but God made you right and He is perfecting you day by day: 'And we, who with unveiled faces all reflect the Lord's glory, are being transformed into his likeness with ever-increasing glory, which comes from the Lord, who is the Spirit' (2 Cor. 3:18).

Fears – such as fear of failure, fear of rejection, fear of change

Fear entered in when Adam and Eve fell into sin in the Garden of Eden: after they had eaten the fruit they were afraid to meet with God and they hid. Fear is a powerful inhibitor, particularly fear of failure, but, viewed positively, failures are no bad thing because we can learn from them – learn to do things a different way. Because we fail in one way or another does not mean that *we* ourselves are failures, although that may be our initial reaction.

Many years ago, sadly, my marriage failed and for some time I told myself that I was a failure. But God lovingly restored me and showed me that, although my marriage had failed, *I* was not a failure. My real sense of worth could only be found in Him and I learned to live differently and experience the reality of God's unconditional love, drawing my worth and security from Him.

'The LORD your God is with you,
    he is mighty to save.

He will take great delight in you,
    he will quiet you with his love,
    he will rejoice over you with singing.' (Zeph. 3:17)

Fear of rejection is a powerful force for many of us – fear that our ideas may be rejected or, even worse, that we personally will be rejected. Undeniably, rejection is painful but it need not be destructive if we are drawing our worth, not from people's appraisal of us, but from who we are *in Christ Jesus*. We are 'chosen by God and precious to him' and 'like living stones, are being built into a spiritual house to be a holy priesthood, offering spiritual sacrifices acceptable to God through Jesus Christ' (1 Pet. 2:4–5). How can we call ourselves failures in the light of such an identity and calling!

Think of the man Jesus told us about in the story of the talents in Matthew 25:14–30, the man to whom his lord gave one talent which he hid in the ground. When the lord returned and asked him what he had done, the man said, 'I was afraid, and went and hid your talent in the ground. Look, there you are.' Fear stopped him multiplying his talent and fear stops us multiplying our talents.

How can we overcome our fears? The answer is love, God's perfect love: 'There is no fear in love; but perfect love casts out fear, because fear involves torment. But he who fears has not been made perfect in love' (1 John 4:18, NKJV).

Fear may arise many times when we are adventuring with God but He will help us overcome those fears and move on.

Unawareness of our gifting

God has uniquely gifted every person but, sadly, few people view themselves as 'gifted'. Find out what your gifts are, perhaps with the help of CWR's 'Discovering Your Basic Gift' chart, or the book *5 Insights to Discovering Your Place in the Body of Christ* by Selwyn

Hughes.[4] In exercising your gifts you will achieve maximum effectiveness with minimum weariness.

Paul tells Timothy, and it applies equally to us, 'Do not neglect the gift that is in you' (1 Tim. 4:14, NKJV). If you don't know what your gifts are, the temptation may be to look at others' gifts and strive for them. In envying others, you may overlook the gifts God has most certainly placed in *you*.

The key word in this scripture is *neglect*, which conveys the idea of being careless with something, not valuing it properly. That is a danger for each of us. We estimate the number of people we can influence or impact and it seems insignificant. We get our priorities wrong and devalue what God is doing in our lives. But the Lord challenges us not to despise 'the day of small things' (Zech. 4:10).

Family responsibilities

God requires us to give our families a higher priority than any work we may do for the Lord. But there are many things we can do without neglecting our family responsibilities.

A woman I know of, a uniquely gifted teacher, is a prime example of using a gift at all stages in life. From being a young mother teaching God's Word to her own children, she went on, as an employer in a business, to train her workers and also introduce them to Jesus. From leading small-group Bible studies in her church she embarked, later in life, as a widow, on a national teaching ministry. Throughout the years the focus of her ministry changed and enlarged, but she faithfully used the gifts and opportunities God had given her.

You too have been gifted for a purpose, '… fan into flame the gift of God, which is in you … ' (2 Tim. 1:6). Use it, nurture it and thank Him for it and you will see the growth, progress and consequent ministry that flows in and through your life and that of your family.

'Do not neglect the gift that is in you … Meditate on these things; give yourself entirely to them, that your progress may be evident to all' (1 Tim. 4:14–15).

How can we move out?

Ask God how you can serve Him right now. Ask Him to show you what's right in front of you and then *do* it. Be willing to do something, however small. Lots of people do nothing because they can't do everything. But God uses seemingly small things to build His kingdom in a most mysterious and exciting way. Some may never have experienced a spiritual 'spring' in terms of a project for the Word. Once released in one area, we can move on to another. The key is to *begin*.

Begin somewhere, perhaps just with 'a smile for Jesus'. Never mind 'entertaining', give hospitality, which can be just a simple meal of soup, fresh bread and cheese, the sort of meal that Jesus probably loved to share with his friends. Consider:

- Can you offer friendship to your neighbours?

- When was the last time you invited non-Christians into your home?

- Is there a prayer group you can join?

- Where could you offer some practical help?

Learn to listen to the voice of God

If we want to hear from God and receive His direction in our lives it's crucial that we learn to listen to His voice. Many times in the Bible the phrase 'He that hath ears to hear, let him hear' is used (eg, Matt. 11:15, KJV). Jesus spoke of what He had heard from the Father:

'I have much to say in judgment of you. But he who sent me is reliable, and what I have heard from him I tell the world' (John 8:26). Jesus' words refer to the intimate relationship He enjoyed with His Father, communing with Him while He was here on earth. God wants those who speak for Him on earth today to have the same kind of relationship with Him, hearing and understanding His heart in the Word He has given us so that we may minister in His name into the lives of others.

Take courage

Very often I have been asked to do something and have not felt equal to the task but, in obedience to God, I have said 'yes' and gone forward in faith. Accordingly, God has used my willingness to develop me and has graciously given me many opportunities to share with women around the world. From my own experience I can testify to 'him who is able to do immeasurably more than all we ask or imagine, according to his power that is at work within us' and say 'to him be glory in the church and in Christ Jesus throughout all generations, for ever and ever! Amen' (Eph. 3:20–21).

Today I want to encourage you, that is, I want to give you courage for the many difficulties, joys and trials you may be facing in your everyday life. There is nothing lacking in you because God is at work in you and there is no lack in Him. With Him, you can do it!

God said to Joshua, 'Be strong and of good courage' (Josh. 1:9). Courage is not a matter of human grit and determination. Courage embraces failure and breathes victory into it. Courage redeems the defeats and failures of the past and uses them as a foundation upon which to build future successes. Courage is rooted in certainty that 'The LORD is faithful to all his promises …' (Psa. 145:13).

Joshua's destiny was in God's hands and God gave him the courage he needed. Where and how do we find such courage? By trusting God as we venture beyond our capabilities or inclinations. Through faith – which is doing it *without* the courage!

Those things He calls you to do, He enables you to do: 'The one who calls you is faithful and he will do it' (1 Thess. 5:24).

Questions for reflection

■ Is there 'something' that you sense God may be wanting you to do? Pray about it and ask God to bring it clearly into focus.

■ How do you respond when faced with a new and challenging opportunity? Do you trust God to equip and enable you to fulfil His calling? What makes it difficult and what might help you to trust Him more? Try to be honest about your thoughts and feelings.

■ Does your way of reading the Bible give you the resources you need for daily living? How might you get more from this manual for living that God has given us? Choose some Bible passages and try meditating on them as I have described.[5] What difference does this approach make?

■ What stops you from moving forward with God? Is it your view of God or of yourself? Is it fear and, if so, what is it that you are most afraid of? Is it something else? Ask God to give you insight into your 'inhibitors'.

■ What particular gifts has God given you? Don't allow yourself to answer 'none'! If you have trouble identifying them, ask others to tell you what they think. Use the chart or the book I have mentioned, to help you.

Notes

1. *Cover to Cover – God's People* by Selwyn Hughes and Trevor J. Partridge (CWR, 2000).
2. *Cover to Cover – Getting the Best from the Bible* by Selwyn Hughes will help you to develop this practice (CWR, 2001).
3. *The Lion, the Witch and the Wardrobe* by C.S. Lewis (Collins, 2001).
4. *5 Insights to Discovering your Place in the Body of Christ*, by Selwyn Hughes (CWR), which you can obtain direct from CWR, from the online store at www.cwrstore.org.uk or from Christian bookshops.
5. See note 2.

Chapter Four

Summer

Beverley Shepherd

'This is to my Father's glory, that you bear much fruit,
showing yourselves to be my disciples … You did not
choose me, but I chose you and appointed you to go and
bear fruit – fruit that will last.'

(John 15:8,16)

What comes to mind when you hear the word 'summer'? I picture the sun shining, the garden in full bloom, long days and warm evenings. Summer as a season of the Spirit is a time of fruitfulness, and this fruitfulness is our Christian calling, flowing from our redemption and ongoing relationship with God.

Yet, when the Lord called me into 'summer' I was reluctant to respond. I was afraid of the exposure. Just as too much exposure to the sun can cause our skin to burn, so I was frightened of being too visible – of being in the line of fire from those who would be critical. There was also fear that the fruit would not be of quality – perhaps I had not drunk in sufficient of the richness of winter, or grown in the most appropriate ways during spring. This may say more about me than about the season, for just as some individuals' skin burns easily and others go wonderfully brown in seconds, so we can respond differently to our spiritual summer. My prayer partner positively bounds towards summer like Tigger in *Winnie the Pooh*, with energy and excitement for all that the season holds. Her response is appropriate as summer is the God-given time for us to fulfil our calling to bear fruit.

'I am the true vine, and my Father is the gardener. He cuts off every branch in me that bears no fruit, while every branch that does bear fruit he prunes so that it will be even more fruitful. You are already clean because of the word I have spoken to you. Remain in me, and I will remain in you. No branch can bear fruit by itself; it must remain in the vine. Neither can you bear fruit unless you remain in me.

'I am the vine; you are the branches. If a man remains in me and I in him, he will bear much fruit; apart from me you can do nothing … This is to my Father's glory, that you bear much fruit, showing yourselves to be my disciples … You did not choose me, but I chose you and appointed you to go and bear fruit – fruit that will last.'

(John 15:1–5,8,16)

Appointed to bear fruit

We see from John 15 that fruitfulness is our clear calling and appointment (v.16). God's purpose in our lives is that we are to be fruit-bearers – fruit is not an optional extra! Fruit does not come from striving or from our own talents and abilities, it comes from abiding (John 15:4). The quality of the fruit depends on the seasons that have gone before – from our times of 'winter' and 'spring'. Jesus, in cursing the fig tree (in Mark 11) is quite clear that growth without fruit is unacceptable. In this instance the fig tree represents the Temple, where there is much outward show of activity but no inner reality. Our lives can look dynamic and full but Jesus is not interested in our activity: His call is to be fruitful. We cannot strive to bear fruit – we can only aim to abide, because fruit comes from abiding or 'remaining'.

As we trace the biblical story of our creation and redemption, we see that God has always intended us to be fruitful. Initially, in Genesis 1:22; 9:1; 35:11, the command to be fruitful refers to having children. The beginning of the book of Psalms (1:3) reminds us that, as we delight ourselves in the law of the Lord, so we shall yield fruit in season. Jeremiah 17:7–8 is a promise that we will never fail to bear fruit if we trust in the Lord and place our confidence in Him alone:

Blessed is the [woman] who trusts in the LORD, whose confidence is in him. [She] will be like a tree planted by the water that sends out its roots by the stream. It does not fear when heat comes; its leaves are always green. It has no worries in a year of drought and never fails to bear fruit.

That Jesus expects us to be fruitful is quite clear from His reaction to those who are not: 'The axe is already at the root of the trees, and every tree that does not produce good fruit will be cut down and thrown into the fire' (Luke 3:9). Summer is not a season apart, it is the consequence of winter and spring – of how deep our roots are in God. Just as we can identify an orange tree by the oranges it bears in summer, so we should be able to identify a Christian by Christian fruit.

Types of fruit

It is very easy to fall into guilt when we see fruit in the lives of others but are unable to identify it in our own life. What fruit should we be looking for? I believe we should look for fruit in three areas – our character, our work and our communities.

Character

Godly character is evidenced by the fruit of the Spirit: love, joy, peace, patience, kindness, goodness, faithfulness, gentleness and self-control (Gal. 5:22). James also sees fruit in terms of godly wisdom: 'But the wisdom that comes from heaven is first of all pure; then peace-loving, considerate, submissive, full of mercy and good fruit, impartial and sincere' (James 3:17). Hosea speaks of the fruit of unfailing love (Hosea 10:12). Throughout our lives, God's intention is to change us more and more into the likeness of His Son.

Work

In Colossians 1, Paul says that not only will the gospel bear fruit (v.6), but also lives that please God will bear fruit in every good work (v.10). He expects fruit in his own life too: 'If I am to go on living in the body, this will mean fruitful labour for me' (Phil. 1:22). Winning souls is also fruit we should look for (Prov. 11:30).

Communities

'Justice will dwell in the desert and righteousness live in the fertile field. The fruit of righteousness will be peace; the effect of righteousness will be quietness and confidence for ever. My people will live in peaceful dwelling-places, in secure homes, in undisturbed places of rest' (Isa. 32:16–18). This paints a picture of communities where, because God's people are righteous, they know His protection and peace. John Stott says, 'Don't blame the meat for going rotten, blame the salt!' In other words, if our communities are 'rotten' then we need to question the effectiveness of our role as salt and light.

In the Old Testament in particular, we see that one of the blessings God gives to His people is fruitfulness in reproduction (Exod. 1:7; Psa. 128:3).

Genuine fruit

This fruit has to bear the hallmark of the manufacturer – godliness. The Bible tells us that godly fruit is 'good' fruit and fruit that will last. There is a danger that we will mistake activity for fruit.

Good fruit

Good fruit reflects God's character; it bears witness to its source. Because of this, people will look and give thanks to the originator – God (Matt. 5:16).

When I worked in the airfreight industry I had particular responsibility for the transportation of clothing from all over Europe to North America. The customs documents that had to be completed were exacting in terms of the amount of detail they wanted about 'country of origin'. Manufacturers had to specify exactly what percentage of the item had been manufactured in which country – difficult if the buttons were made in one place, the fabric in another and it was sewn together in a third! Good fruit only has one country of origin: 'Made in heaven' – it originates with God and not in our own sinful natures.

Lasting fruit

This fruit will last into eternity (Matt. 6:19–21) and survive the day of testing without being burned up (1 Cor. 3:10–15). On holiday in Turkey one year, I visited a carpet factory. A pleasant afternoon was spent drinking apple tea and viewing myriad different carpets. They differed not only in size and design but also in the materials used. My eye was caught by a small silk carpet – it was absolutely beautiful. Apparently there were many fake silk carpets to be found in the markets and the salesman informed me that I could tell the genuine article through testing it by fire – pure silk carpets would not burn up! On the day of testing, will our fruit be shown to be genuine?

In industry I see many projects, that people have poured endless time and money into, get scrapped at the last moment – cut down before they could bear any fruit. If only businesses knew in advance which projects would be of lasting value then they would be more effective and less wasteful of resources. Similarly in our lives, we need divine guidance to know where to invest our time and energy, we need to 'work with God' and not 'for Him' – then we can expect there to be lasting fruit. Note though, that we have to entrust the fruitfulness to God – we may not see some of it in our lifetimes.

The alternatives

1. Bad fruit that does not last

What makes fruit bad? Hosea 10:13 tells us that it is a matter of origin – when the origin is ourselves and not God. God will not brook counterfeit and so will show the fruit for what it is – fake.

A friend of mine made a business trip to the Far East and bought himself a very chunky gold fake Rolex watch. Imagine his delight when he walked into a jeweller in England and the assistant remarked on his watch, saying that he wished he could afford a watch worth several thousand pounds. My friend informed the assistant that it had only cost £5! Several weeks later, though, the 'gold' started to flake off and his wrist went green. Just as with cheap counterfeit goods, the poor quality of our 'bad' fruit will eventually show through. Works done in our own strength, when tested by fire, will be shown to be straw.

2. No fruit

There could be several reasons why there is no fruit:

- The wrong season
- Hard or infertile soil
- An immature plant
- The plant is diseased or wilted
- The plant is dead

Wrong season

Just as in my garden I do not expect my apple tree to bear apples during December, so there may be no spiritual fruit because it isn't the right season. It might be more appropriate to say 'no visible fruit' for, as we have seen, the fruit of winter tends to be in character rather than in works. Too often we strive to grow visible fruit in winter when God is asking us to grow our roots.

Hard or infertile soil

I had the privilege of listening to an experienced missionary talk about the years he had spent overseas. He mentioned the difference in 'observable fruit' when based in two different locations. In one, the hard ground had been 'broken up' by the work and prayers of the missionaries who had been there before him, and it had been well watered by their tears for the lost. As a result, his ministry had much demonstrable fruit. In the second country, where he had worked just as hard and sought God just as much, the fruit was far less evident because the ground was hard. He knew that his work was to prepare the ground for future missionaries, just as others had done for him previously. The true fruit of his labours would not be seen for years, perhaps even generations to come.

Immature plant

Whilst on a church weekend led by a Methodist minister friend of mine, I was very struck by an exercise he asked us to complete. We were to draw three pictures representing some aspect of our relationship with God. One of my pictures (though my drawing skills hardly merit that title) was of God as the gardener, pruning back a plant. Instead of drawing, as I had intended, God cutting back one of the leafy stems, I drew Him cutting off the flower. In checking this with a gardening friend I was told that gardeners sometimes do this with young plants to prevent them bearing fruit that year so that all the strength goes into enabling them to bear more fruit the next year. In the church we can throw young Christians in at the deep end and then they often burn out quickly because they were not nurtured and strengthened before being expected to bear fruit.

Diseased or wilted plants

Summer can be very hot and dry and so plants need plenty of watering. We too can wilt during our spiritual summer through over busyness and not spending enough time in both physical rest or in drinking in from God's Word. Even when Jesus had a packed programme we see Him getting up early to pray (eg Mark 1:35), in order to know God's direction and be sustained by Him. Sometimes we can become sick through exhaustion or feel choked by cares and worries, because we have failed to get adequate sleep or to entrust our cares to God.

Dead plants

Dead plants produce no fruit! In the garden it is often obvious when a plant is dead. For us, however, we may look alive while in reality our spirits feel dead. This may be the result of disappointment or disobedience. The words of the angel of the church in Sardis are a warning to us: 'I know your deeds; you have a reputation of being alive, but you are dead' (Rev. 3:1).

The good news is that God can grow the young, strengthen the weak, heal the sick and raise the dead!

Beware the weeds!

As any gardener will tell you, weeding is one of the summer chores! Weeds have all the same nutritional and cultivational requirements as the plants we want, and so compete hungrily with them for available food and moisture. The weeds that are most likely to appear in our spiritual garden during summer are self-sufficiency, self-idolatry and self-depreciation.

Self-sufficiency

In the busyness of summer it is easy to fall back on our own skills and abilities rather that to seek God's supply. In summer we have the opportunity to use our skills, experience and gifting – and in many aspects of our work we know what it is to be competent and play to our strengths. It can, therefore, be hard to trust God when it is quicker and easier to trust ourselves!

This was brought home to me in a rate negotiation with a key client. I had prayed about it, yet my prayer was of the 'delegation' variety: 'Lord, you know the rate I want to achieve, please get it for me!' Gradually the Lord began to impress on me that His way was different – I was to go to my client and tell them, up front, that any rate they chose to give me was OK with me! 'Lord, you don't understand – you just don't negotiate that way! Trust me Lord, I train courses in this stuff – this isn't how you do it!' The Lord answered: 'Trust in the LORD with all your heart and lean not on your own understanding … Do not be wise in your own eyes' (Prov. 3:5–7). It was hard, and I knew that if I didn't say something at the beginning of the meeting I never would, so I told the training manager that he was free to decide the rate and I would accept his decision. His reaction was extraordinary. He had been in a meeting earlier that day with a trainer who had pushed him for a rate that he did not feel he could afford – he had agreed the rate, but decided to give that trainer no further work. As a result of my stance in the negotiation, together with my track record, I was made their 'trainer of choice' and was given my pick of every training project! (The rate agreed was good too!) The decision to trust God more than our own abilities, skills and experience is a daily, sometimes hourly, decision.

Self-idolatry

In summer there is the danger that we see the fruit and think it is the result of our own skill and work. 'You may say to yourself, "My power and the strength of my hands have produced this wealth for me." But remember the LORD your God, for it is he who gives you the ability to produce wealth, and so confirms his covenant, which he swore to your forefathers, as it is today' (Deut. 8:17–18). We end up congratulating ourselves rather than giving thanks to God. There is also a danger that we worship the 'fruit' rather than the God who enabled us to produce it. The way to 'pull up' this weed is thankfulness. Learn to thank God in all circumstances: 'Praise the LORD, O my soul, and forget not all his benefits' (Psa. 103:2).

Self-depreciation

The belief that God cannot use 'me' is both limiting the omnipotence of God and calling Him a liar. God designed us to be fruit-bearers and to believe otherwise is a false humility. In fact, God puts it more strongly:

> [Sisters], think of what you were when you were called. Not many of you were wise by human standards; not many were influential; not many were of noble birth. But God chose the foolish things of the world to shame the wise; God chose the weak things of the world to shame the strong. He chose the lowly things of this world and the despised things – and the things that are not – to nullify the things that are, so that no-one may boast before him.' (1 Cor. 1:26–29)

There is no one that God cannot use!

There may be times in our lives, however, when God will not use us because we are not clean. 'In a large house there are articles not only of gold and silver, but also of wood and clay; some are for noble purposes and some for ignoble. If a man cleanses himself from the latter, he will be an instrument for noble purposes, made holy, useful to the Master and prepared to do any good work' (2 Tim. 2:20–21). The main qualification for usefulness is cleanliness. I was attending a Christian conference during a time of deliberate rebellion in one area of my life. Due to a mix-up in communication another speaker was talking on the subject that I considered to be 'my' area. I did not mind this as I thought it would give me the opportunity to learn from someone else. When he wasn't very good (in my view!), I questioned the Lord as to the reasons why I was not giving the talk. His gentle, humbling and incisive reply was, 'Beverley, I would have loved you to give a talk at this conference but you were not clean enough for use.'

Learn to enter summer with joyfulness and anticipation, knowing that you are called to bear fruit. Be quick to pull up the weeds of self-sufficiency, self-idolatry and self-depreciation. Keep short accounts with the Lord so that you are always ready for use and remember to drink in His loving supply on a continual basis so that you don't dry out and wilt!

Questions for reflection

- How do you feel about the spiritual season of summer?

- What does being 'appointed to bear fruit' mean for you?

- What fruit are you aware of in your character, your work and your community?

- Why might there not be fruit in your life at present?

- In what areas are you tempted to self-sufficiency?

- In what areas are you tempted to self-idolatry?

- In what areas are you tempted to self-depreciation? (Ask God to show you.)

Chapter Five

Autumn

Jeannette Barwick

'Be patient, then, brothers, until the Lord's coming.
See how the farmer waits for the land to yield its
valuable crop and how patient he is for the autumn
and spring rains.'

(James 5:7)

Autumn is often the most beautiful of seasons, a time when God's creation shows forth in all its glory, but it is also a time of 'ending', as fruitfulness ceases and the leaves fall, stripped from their branches by strong winds. All these signs herald the winter which must follow. There is late fruit which comes in the autumn – the last of the tomatoes and the beans, the apples that needed the late summer rain to swell the fruit. There is fruit to be had but it is not prolific like the main summer harvest. Patience and perseverance are required: 'Be patient, then, brothers, until the Lord's coming. See how the farmer waits for the land to yield its valuable crop and how patient he is for the autumn and spring rains' (James 5:7). So it is for us also that patience and perseverance are needed in a spiritual 'autumn'.

Reviewing and pruning

Season of mists and mellow fruitfulness.

(John Keats, *Ode to Autumn*)

I live overlooking a riverbank where several weeping willow trees grow and, autumn by autumn, I see these trees seemingly 'slaughtered' as the year draws towards its end. But, with the spring, comes profuse new growth – the willows come to life again, more beautiful and graceful than before. So, in our spiritual autumn, we need to review our activities, with a mind to the future, radically pruning back anything which is unfruitful.

'I am the true vine, and my Father is the gardener. He cuts off every branch in me that bears no fruit, while every branch that does bear fruit he prunes, so that it will be even more fruitful.'

(John 15:1–2)

Practically, allowing the Divine Gardener's work in our life may mean laying down a work we may have been doing for a significant period of time. As we review, we must realise that we do not need to keep doing things the way we have always done them. What's important is to decide on the best way ahead for the future of the work.

Jesus used many analogies to teach us the truths of the kingdom. One of these was the lesson of the seed grain, in which He compared the life of the believer to the process of development of a grain of wheat. 'Unless a grain of wheat falls to the ground and dies,' He said, 'it remains only a single seed. But if it dies, it produces many seeds' (John 12:24). This process, often painful, is the same one we must go through if we are to continue to bear fruit.

In honest hearts, committed to the fulfilment of God's purposes, the Holy Spirit works, sometimes mysteriously. At each stage of growth, if there is to be a fuller development in the future, there has to be a casting off of much that was necessary before. The danger lies in our clinging to old experiences, old helps and old supports, when the Spirit-life within is pressing us forward to another stage – especially likely if the way forward appears to lead 'downward' instead of 'upward'.

As I have pursued these thoughts, I have been reminded of my very dear friend Olivia Kyambadde in Kampala, Uganda. I saw her on a visit to Uganda when she was just coming out of such a 'grain of wheat' experience and I know she is happy for me to share her story with you.

Olivia had lived a comfortable and fruitful life. She has four children and for many years her husband worked for an oil company. She came to Waverley in 1993 to train on the Institute in Christian Counselling, having saved the money for her fare over several years by making wedding cakes and leasing her car for hire. When she returned to Kampala she established a counselling service at Kampala Pentecostal Church, a very large church based in an old converted concrete cinema. It is a simple building but, with its thousands of members, it throbs with the life of Christ. Olivia is highly respected and very much part of this wonderful church, one which reaches out to the community, especially to the hundreds of orphaned children who live in the children's villages created specifically for them. It was for the care and support of the children's mothers in these villages that she became responsible.

When her husband retired early, they embarked on a new venture, to create a purpose-built Christian Retreat Centre. It was, when completed, a beautiful place for ministry. Olivia's mother, in failing health, lived with them for seven years, needing total care, which she was glad to give.

Problems began when her second daughter, at university in Kampala, got into bad company. Then a business in which her husband was a partner failed and the financial difficulties that ensued required them to close and sell the Retreat Centre and move to a rented flat. It was decided that their daughter should transfer to the university in Nairobi, Kenya, and during the two days Olivia was away settling her in there, her mother died. In a short space of time, the family had lost their lovely home and furniture and their financial security, and Olivia was bereft of much that she held dear. Her tears flowed daily for many months but she submitted herself to the Lord's love and mercy.

Having come through such an experience, Olivia is able now to see how God is using all of that to bring blessing and build an even more fruitful ministry. Her daughter did well at the university in Nairobi and her husband, having worked from their home in the flat for three years to make a living for the family, now holds the executive position of Business Manager at Kampala Pentecostal Church. The

Lord opened a door of opportunity for Olivia to train the police, regarded widely then as the 'lowest of the low', and she received the full support of her church leadership to undertake this. So effective has this training been that an annual Police Appreciation Day is now held every 28th day of February, to which many of the city dignitaries are invited.[1]

This is what Olivia said to me: 'I could never have done the work the Lord has led me into now as I was before.' She and her training team, Harmony, contribute to every course run at the two police training schools in the country, teaching on ethics, morals and relationships, coming alongside and supporting the officers in training. They have even worked with the traffic police to run team days for the hundreds of taxi drivers and bike riders in the capital. Their input into teaching people why they do the things they do is really helping to strengthen and build up respect for that nation's police force.

What can be learned from Olivia's experience is that God cannot fully use a person who is not broken and completely surrendered to Him. Without such brokenness he or she may become proud and arrogant in doing God's work. The heart of a person who has been broken resists pride.

Olivia also confessed to me: 'I used to think that, if people got into debt or financial difficulty, it was their own fault. How differently I understand this kind of situation now. God has brought me into contact with people whose lives are so troubled and messed up. I know I could never have come alongside them as I do, if I had not gone through these five years of trouble myself.'

Yes, Olivia experienced great loss, but she is both tender and strong in her new ministry.

The gain of suffering is reflected in Paul's prayer, 'Thank God … that he is our Father and the source of all mercy and comfort. For he

gives us comfort in all our trials so that we in turn may be able to give the same sort of strong sympathy to others in their troubles ...'
(2 Cor. 1:3–4, Phillips).

Our experience of loss may be very different to Olivia's but, as we accept God's pruning by letting go of past fruitful works and allowing Him to move us on, there will be a sense of loss. It is important that we don't deny the reality of that loss or pretend not to feel it.

If our sense of identity is bound up in our work for God rather than in God Himself, then that sense of loss will be more acute.

Where do you find your identity? Do you think of yourself as a wife, a mother, daughter, sister, nurse, teacher, company director, pastoral worker, chairman of the missionary committee? These are all roles that you play but they are not who *you* are. Monitor your motives and focus on *being* rather than doing. If any of these are the source from which you are drawing your identity and purpose then, if anything happens to your job, your position in the church or the people around you, you will be devastated. If however, instead, you are drawing your life from Christ, you will be affected, feel disappointed and sad, no doubt, but you will be able to go on. Like Paul you will be able to say,

> We are hard pressed on every side, but not crushed; perplexed, but not in despair; persecuted, but not abandoned; struck down, but not destroyed. We always carry around in our body the death of Jesus, so that the life of Jesus may also be revealed in our body ...
> (2 Cor. 4:8–10)

Let's look for a moment at an experience common to many women. What happens when our children are grown? Do we thrill at their blooming and see it as an opportunity to move forward? I hope so, but first we may experience the 'empty nest syndrome' – the painful feelings and the accompanying sense of loss that is part of that autumn phase of our lives.

Other people, things and responsibilities can absorb our attention in a way that keeps us from seeing the Lord in His full majesty. Remember what Isaiah said: 'In the year that King Uzziah died, I saw the Lord sitting on a throne, high and exalted, and the train of his robe filled the temple' (Isa. 6:1).

King Uzziah was a good king. People respected him and he ruled in a good and righteous way, but all the while Uzziah was alive and reigning Isaiah did not focus fully on God. When the king died, Isaiah could rest his gaze on God, he was free to respond to the call of God on His life. We, like him, can allow so many things to take our gaze away from God. It's an arresting thought that even a small coin held close to the eye can blot out the huge and powerful light of the sun.

Investing in others

It is a clear command in Scripture to invest in the next generation.

> … we will tell the next generation
> the praiseworthy deeds of the LORD,
>   his power, and the wonders he has done.
> … he commanded our forefathers
>   to teach their children,
> so that the next generation
>   would know them … (Psa. 78:4–6a)

Paul instructs Titus to ensure that the older women in the church train the younger women (Titus 2:3–4).

Notice that it is not the elders who are to train the young women. I've heard it said that the instruction was to stop the young women leading the men astray and indeed I've talked to all too many ministers' wives distressed by the young women taking up their husbands' time and attention. Marriages are safer if younger women are counselled by the older women rather than the pastor or elders. Paul was spiritually astute and knew that women need women yet the ministry of older women teaching is, regrettably, not practised very widely in churches today.

The 'in' word for investing in others these days is 'mentoring', another way of talking about the command to be the example further down the path: she made it – I can too.

Women may give and receive mentoring in a variety of ways. A mother of several children, for instance, can inspire others in the area of motherhood. Then there are those whose marriages provide others, by observation, with effective tools for their own marriages. There are also women who by their passion for the Lord and gift for revelation of the Word, have encouraged others to follow Him more intensely. Christian women have a need for the love, guidance and encouragement of one another.

Investment in others is necessary, not only in the generational sense but also when it involves passing on to our peers the responsibilities that we are laying down. In such situations it is important to communicate principles but avoid producing 'clones'. We should be seeking successors who will bring new gifts and strengths and, importantly, fresh vision for the way ahead.

When I moved on from my full involvement in the OASIS outreach ministry to local mothers and toddlers, to work for CWR, I thought I could continue to be involved in the leadership of the team without being present at the meetings. However, I very quickly saw that such an involvement was impractical and inappropriate. It was time for the team to be given free rein and my role was only to maintain interest and support and to encourage, without further close involvement. Only in this way could the others develop fully and take responsibility. I felt the sense of loss, of course, but I knew this was the right thing to do, for us all.

God's desire is that His people may be prepared for works of service, 'so that the body of Christ may be built up until we all reach unity in the faith and in the knowledge of the Son of God and become mature, attaining to the whole measure of the fullness of Christ' (Eph. 4:12–13).

Let's be mentors who pass the torch on to the next generation, not only through spiritual insights, important though they are, but also by sharing the tools of normal, everyday life.

The greatest investment we can make is in the character of people. That is an investment that goes on and on and affects the generations to come. The smallest investment now can have a big effect on the generations that will follow. It's like this: a small change in direction here, maybe just a one degree turn, can result in someone moving in an entirely different direction further ahead. Just an inch of difference here can mean a mile of difference down the road. The right influence and support to make a righteous decision now can affect the entire course of someone's life.

Ending well

Let it be our goal to 'end well'. This means working specifically towards good conclusions, in terms of relationships as well as projects. Ending projects involves careful planning, good record-keeping, phased hand-over and then really letting go, so that any on-going contact will be appropriate and encouraging but not interfering. With relationships it means fostering openness, trust and consideration.

One day, as we enjoyed cuddling her new baby son, my younger daughter Katy gave me a lovely example of a good ending. She told me what had happened as she visited a previous place of work earlier that day. She had worked with the company for six years, a mutually fruitful time, when she was offered a three-month travel sabbatical on full pay. She took up the offer with great enthusiasm and her husband was allowed unpaid leave so that he could accompany her. In the months leading up to this, there were many changes in the company and things became very difficult. She ended up handing in her three months' notice as she took her leave, which, honourably, the company did not withdraw. When she returned, she took up employment elsewhere. In her field of work there are restraints on contact with former clients and colleagues. Misunderstandings arose, unfounded allegations were made and solicitors' letters ensued, but Katy was determined to try to resolve the misunderstandings that had occurred and restore the relationship. She kept in regular contact with her former employers, doing all she could to put things right and maintain openness, and was thrilled, on visiting them to show off baby Joshua, to be received warmly, as they expressed genuine pleasure for her in her new work and phase of life as a young mother. 'I'm so glad I persevered, Mum!' she said. Perseverance – and commitment – are key words if we, like Katy, are to 'end well'.

There are some relationships that must change or end through breakdown or death. I want to spend a little time thinking about ending well in relationships outside of work or church. When, to my great sadness, my own marriage broke down some 25 years ago, I was determined, under God, to forgive my husband and we were both committed to doing all that we could to protect our daughters from as much further harm as possible. Through a deeply painful time we persevered, and we have retained a relationship that is free from bitterness and has at its heart respect and affection that is wholesome for our children and grandchildren. Although the marriage ended in breakdown, we did all that we could to end well.

Death that is expected, hard as it may be, can also give us the opportunity to end well. I was blessed in having the opportunity to say what I wanted to say to both my parents as they came to the end of their days with us. I thank God for the comfort that gave me.

My friend Edwina comes to my mind in this context. Just ten days after she had attended the first Seasons of the Spirit weekend, her husband suffered a stroke at home, followed rapidly by another in hospital, and special nursing care was required until he died four months later. They were painful and challenging months for Edwina, but her reliance was on God for this season of her marriage, and she found herself amazingly prepared through the teaching and fellowship the weekend had given her. Key phrases came back to her which, as you read, may become key phrases for you. Her desire to 'persevere' and 'end well' kept her looking to God for the love, grace and wisdom she needed. Not only were family relationships healed and restored during this time, but a special friendship was forged with a neighbour who prayed and walked with her through the valley of the shadow.

Many of you may have experienced difficult or fractured relationships and found that, despite every effort on your part, restoration has not been possible. I can only encourage you to seek God's help in ending as well as you can.

> Get rid of all bitterness, rage and anger, brawling and slander, along with every form of malice. Be kind and compassionate to one another, forgiving each other, just as in Christ God forgave you. (Eph. 4:31–32)

Perseverance

Our spiritual autumn gives us time for reflection, the opportunity to revisit failures and, in so doing, relinquish regrets and redefine our values. As we reflect on the past we can take time to rethink our priorities. Reality must be faced so that we can look back honestly and make any adjustment needed before we undergo transition from one season to the next. We need patience and perseverance, but this can be a rich time of inner growth.

In terms of my work with CWR, I find myself in an autumn season, seeking God's help in making changes in my working life and redefining my role for the future. My goal is to have more time with my family and to be free to give myself more fully to the ministry to women. I'm doing all that I can to end well, engaging in a process of reviewing, cutting back and pruning the work with my colleagues so that new growth may take place and good fruit be borne in the coming years. We are looking to God, trusting that the ministry to women will continue, develop and grow.

The seasons of our lives are appointed by God. As we allow ourselves to experience them, in all the challenges and possibilities they present, may we draw ever closer to Him.

But I trust in you, O LORD;
    I say, 'You are my God.'
My times are in your hands. (Psa. 31:14–15a)

Questions for reflection

■ Is there something God is asking you to lay aside or to 'prune'?
What might this involve?

■ Thinking of Isaiah, are there things in your life that are good in
themselves but may be taking your gaze away from God? How has
God used painful experiences of loss or ending to bring blessing
and fruitfulness to you?

■ What would you find most difficult to be asked to part with? Why
do you think this is so? Try to be really honest.

■ In what way do you invest in others? Are there ways that you
could invest more? What stops you from investing in others?

■ Thinking of endings in your life, are there things for which you
need to seek God's forgiveness – and the forgiveness of others? Or
are there, perhaps, blessings for which you have not thanked Him
sufficiently? Ask God to help you confront reality and bring about
restoration where necessary. If restoration is not possible, what
might help you to move on with God?

■ Is perseverance difficult for you? What makes you give up or what
helps you to keep going? What might help you to grow spiritually
in this vital aspect of Christian living?

Notes
1. A fuller account of Olivia's story may be found in *Transformed Lives*, published by CWR.

Chapter Six

Living in the Light of Eternity

Jeannette Barwick

Original sessions were given by Beth Clark and Nicky-Sue Leonard.
In compiling this chapter, I have been helped greatly by Selwyn
Hughes' book, *Heaven Bound*.[1]

'… an inheritance that can never perish, spoil or fade –
kept in heaven for you …'

(1 Peter 1:4)

The lives of the great saints of the past reveal an important truth. They were able to persevere, or to 'keep on keeping on', because, through the various seasons of their lives, they lived in the light of eternity. In whatever situations they found themselves, the great and the godly always seemed able to keep heaven in view. How can we, in our times, learn to live this way too?

Some think that a preoccupation with heaven will lead us to become 'so heavenly minded that we are no earthly good'. However, as history shows, some of the greatest social reformers, such as John Wesley, William Booth and Lord Shaftesbury, were 'God-intoxicated' men whose perspective on life extended to heaven and who worked all the better down here because of it. It is not 'other worldly' to talk and think and look forward to heaven, provided that heaven is not all we think about. 'The happiest people on earth,' someone has said, 'are those who keep their eyes focused on heaven.' And the psalmist wrote, 'In thy presence is fulness of joy; at thy right hand there are pleasures for evermore' (Psa. 16:11, KJV). When we get to heaven, joy will be found through realisation but it can be found right now, to some degree at least, by anticipation.

Malcolm Muggeridge, in his book *Jesus Rediscovered*, said that ever since he was a boy he had sensed that he was a stranger in this world and that there was a world beyond this to which he was ever moving. He wrote, 'The only ultimate disaster that can befall us, I have come to realise, is to feel ourselves to be at home here on earth. As long as we are aliens we cannot forget our true homeland.'

The apostle Paul said in his letter to the Philippians that, as far as heaven was concerned, he was eager to go but willing to stay here on earth for their sake (Phil. 1:23). Most Christians, if we are honest, would put that the other way round: willing to go to heaven but eager to stay here.

A pastor, one Sunday morning, asked the children in his

congregation this question: 'How many of you want to go to heaven?' Everyone raised their hands except one little boy at the back. 'You don't want to go to heaven when you die?' the pastor queried. 'Oh, when I die?' said the little boy. 'I thought you meant right now!'

Heaven now?

So why is it that we don't hanker after heaven? One reason, I think, is that we become so much engrossed with the things of time that they blot out the reality of eternity.

Returning to the great saints of the past, one perceives that, although they enjoyed material things, they did not crave them in a way that many do today, but gave them a minor place in their lives. The trappings of life were given no more importance than the furnishings of an inn by those who regarded themselves as only staying for a while. With such a 'mindset' and a heart aflame with love and longing for Christ, they could sing:

> This world is not my home, I'm just a-passing through,
> My treasures are laid up somewhere beyond the blue.
> The angels beckon me from heaven's open door
> And I can't feel at home in this world any more.

Another reason why we cling to the idea of earth rather than heaven is that we entertain the foolish notion that we can have heaven now. Some Christians claim that once we are in Christ we can and, in fact, should have health and wealth until the day we die. This is nonsense, of course, and quite unscriptural. Yes, God does answer prayer and He works miracles still. We know of wonderful instances of God providing for people's financial needs in miraculous ways, but He does not act in this way always. Sometimes He lets His people struggle and their prayers remain unanswered. Selwyn Hughes claims that here in this world we experience what he calls 'a marred joy', meaning that, even at our best moments, we are aware that our current experience is not the fullness of what we were made for. Some would call this 'negative thinking'. In my view, it is realism. And facing reality does not diminish the joy. Rather, it saves us from pretending that what we have is better than it is.

Hope makes the difference

Consider the passage in the apostle Paul's second letter to the Corinthians (4:8–18) that begins with his statement:

> We are hard pressed on every side, yet not crushed; we are perplexed, but not in despair; persecuted, but not forsaken; struck down, but not destroyed … (NKJV)

Paul then goes on to write of the deathly struggles that were part of his condition and, in all of this, it is clear that what steeled him to go forward was keeping heaven in view. In verse 18, in a moment of great exultation, he says, '… we do not look at the things which are seen, but at the things which are not seen' (NKJV).

Paul's theme, continuing into the early part of chapter 5, is that one day he will arrive in heaven where all the struggles and problems of earth will be over for ever and that to be absent from the body is to be present with the Lord.

Critics of Christianity will disdainfully call 'living in the light of eternity' escapism, but that is a word that could never justly be applied to the writings of the great apostle. He faced the reality of heaven so that he might better face the realities of earth.

Throughout the entire history of the Christian Church the people of God, facing life's problems, have drawn great comfort from the promise of heaven. What, for example, helped the slaves of America's

Deep South to endure their afflictions? Snatched from their dwelling places in Africa centuries ago they were transported to America and sold as slaves to plantation owners, some of them merciless brutes. A clue to how they bore their suffering can be found in 'negro spirituals', songs of those times in which a common thread running through was the prospect of heaven. One of the best-known and loved of these is *Swing low sweet chariot, coming for to carry me home* which was composed to comfort those slaves with the assurance of one day being with the Lord Jesus in a world of perfect freedom. I wonder if the thousands who sang this during the 2003 Rugby World Cup, when England triumphantly carried the cup home, had any idea of its origins!

Brent Curtis and John Eldridge in their book, *The Sacred Romance*, say, 'Take away the hope of heaven and our journey is a death march.' The anticipation of heaven provides us with a powerful 'analgesic' enabling us to cope with difficult and painful situations and that is the power of hope. It is like a doctor saying to a woman in labour, 'Hold on! The baby you long for will soon be in your arms. Now you feel pain, but soon there will be delight'. It is surprising how the hope of heaven, although it does not remove the pain of present circumstances, certainly helps to diminish it. Awaiting us in heaven is joy beyond description: as C.S. Lewis wrote in one of his books, 'Joy is the serious business of heaven.'

The promise of joy

Heaven and joy are often linked together in the New Testament, as when Jesus said, '… there is rejoicing in the presence of the angels of God over one sinner who repents' (Luke 15:10). Likewise, in the parable of the talents, Jesus promised that those who use their talents well will hear the Master say, 'Enter into the joy of your lord' (Matt. 25:21, NKJV).

In his first epistle, the apostle John talks about 'the love the Father has lavished on us, that we should be called children of God!' (1 John 3:1). He goes on to say: '… now we are children of God, and what we will be has not yet been made known. But we know that when he appears, we shall be like him, for we shall see him as he is' (v.2).

Whatever work is going on now in our hearts will one day be fulfilled in all its glory. In heaven the seed that is within us will grow to dimensions that are beyond the power of our imagination to conceive. A songwriter expressed it like this:

Just remember in the winter
Far beneath the bitter snows
Lies the seed that with the sun's love
In the spring becomes the rose. [2]

Indeed, 'what we will be has not yet been made known'!

Christians have sometimes asked why, after our conversion, God doesn't take us immediately to be with Him in heaven and thus save us from the perplexities and difficulties of life here on earth. What they don't understand is that the Holy Spirit is with us on our journey to heaven, developing character qualities – the fruit of the Spirit listed in Galatians 5:22 – that enable us to represent to those around us some of those things on which heaven is built. The greatest of these, of course, is love.

Why do we come off the rails?

Some Christians start out for heaven with strong determination but, sadly, are derailed along the way. What are some of the possible reasons for this derailment?

One could be the fact that, for some people, there is, deep down, no real wholeheartedness in following Christ and, after a while, the difficulties they meet generate apathy and indifference. Another could be the matter we have already mentioned: preoccupation with material things. Yet another possibility is the fear of persecution. This can take many forms, from the sort of gentle mockery or marginalisation we sometimes experience in religiously tolerant countries to the very real and even life-threatening form encountered elsewhere. Then, to many people, heaven seems a long way off and the race is arduous, demanding endurance, commitment, determination and self-discipline. What we must never forget, however, is that all the resources of heaven are at our disposal to enable us to persevere. We have a little bit of heaven to go to heaven in.

There will be times on the road to heaven, when, however well-intentioned we are, we will fail, make mistakes and let the Lord down. But how reassuring it is to know that we can always count on God's forgiveness to restore us and to lift us up when we have fallen.

If we confess our sins, He is faithful and just to forgive us our sins and to cleanse us from all unrighteousness. (1 John 1:9, NKJV)

In this there is a clear reminder that, while forgiveness and restoration are always available, they become a reality in our lives only when we truly repent. We must never take them for granted

How to 'keep on keeping on'

Focus on Jesus
Eugene Peterson, in *The Message*, has a wonderful paraphrase of Hebrews 12:1–3:

Do you see what this means – all these pioneers who blazed the way, all these veterans cheering us on? It means we'd better get on with it.

Strip down, start running – and never quit! No extra spiritual fat, no parasitic sins. Keep your eyes on *Jesus*, who both began and finished this race we're in. Study how he did it. Because he never lost sight of where he was headed – that exhilarating finish in and with God – he could put up with anything along the way: cross, shame, whatever. And now he's *there*, in the place of honour, right alongside God. When you find yourselves flagging in your faith, go over that story again, item by item, that long litany of hostility he plowed through. That will shoot adrenaline into your souls!

So, as we focus on how Jesus ran the race, we ourselves are encouraged to follow in His footsteps, realising that in all the difficulties that faced Him, He had us and our salvation in mind.

Spending time in God's Word

Another resource to help us to 'keep on keeping on' is God's Word. Because God has, in a sense, come *into* the Bible, He also comes *out of* it and, as we read His Word, His inspiration passes mysteriously into us. Someone has said that the Bible is inspired because it is inspiring. That does not, of course, wholly explain the inspiration of Scripture but it is most definitely true that the God who inspired the Bible inspires those who spend time in it and so we must make Bible study and meditation a priority in our lives.

Prayer

A third way that we can 'keep on keeping on' is by engaging with God through personal prayer. When we pray it is important to remember that we are entering into a conversation, a two-way process: we are talking to Him but He is also talking to us. This means trying to spend as much time listening as talking, something that does not come easily to many of us.

Christian fellowship

A fourth way to prevent our footsteps flagging is to cultivate friendships with other Christians. Paul encouraged the Colossians to talk together about the Lord, to sing and pray together and share spiritual truths (Col. 3:14–17), and Eugene Peterson gives his own punchy version in *The Message*:

> None of this going off and doing your own thing … Instruct and direct one another using good common sense. And sing, sing your hearts out to God! Let every detail in your lives – words, actions, whatever – be done in the name of the Master, Jesus, thanking God the Father every step of the way.

Commitment

The Methodists have given careful attention to this matter of trusting God in all the seasons of our lives and persevering on the path to heaven. As a member of the Methodist Church myself, I have found the Covenant Service, as it is called, to be a very powerful incentive at the beginning of each new year. It is deeply challenging and spurs me on to commit myself into God's hands in every area of my life and trust Him in the year ahead to lead me into the season of His choosing.

Let me quote it verbatim for those of you who may not know it:

> In the Old Covenant, God chose Israel to be His people and to obey His laws. Our Lord Jesus Christ, by His death and resurrection, has made a New Covenant with all who trust in Him. We stand within this Covenant and we bear His name. On the one side, God promises in this Covenant to give us new life in Christ. On the other side we are pledged to live no more for ourselves but for Him. Beloved in Christ, let us again claim for ourselves this Covenant

which God has made with His people, and take the yoke of Christ upon us. To take His yoke upon us means that we are content that He appoint us our place and work, and that He Himself be our reward.

Christ has many services to be done; some are easy, others are difficult; some bring honour, others bring reproach; some are suitable to our natural inclinations and material interests, others are contrary to both. In some we may please Christ and please ourselves, in others we cannot please Christ except by denying ourselves. Yet the power to do all these things is given us in Christ, who strengthens us. Therefore let us make this Covenant of God our own. Let us give ourselves anew to Him, trusting in His promises and relying on His grace.

Our Response:

Lord God, I am no longer my own, but Yours. Put me to what You will, rank me with whom You will; put me to doing, put me to suffering; let me be employed for You or laid aside for You, exalted for You or brought low for You; let me be full, let me be empty; let me have all things, let me have nothing; I freely and whole-heartedly yield all things to Your pleasure and disposal.

And now, glorious and blessed God, Father, Son and Holy Spirit, You are mine and I am Yours. So be it. And the covenant now made on earth, let it be ratified in heaven. Amen.

Hebrews 11 gives us a long list of men and women who ran the race towards heaven and finished strongly. It has been called 'the Westminster Abbey of the Bible' because it records the names of those, the famous and not so famous, who in the pre-Christian era, walked the path to heaven with confidence and trust in God. Amongst those names are found Abraham and Moses, Sarah and Rahab. Of course, Hebrews 11 is really an unfinished chapter in the sense that, over the centuries, many more names have been and will be added to the long list of heroes of faith. As we take note of the multitude of men who qualify as 'heroes of faith', let us not forget some of the 'heroines of faith' of modern times, women who qualify equally for their place in God's Hall of Fame. Amongst the women of recent times who have inspired me personally are Mother Teresa, Joni Eareckson Tada, Corrie Ten Boom and Ruth Graham Bell. Elizabeth Elliott is another great woman: she went back to minister among the same tribe in South America who killed her missionary husband, Jim. Jackie Pullinger, too, has inspired thousands worldwide through her ministry to drug addicts in Hong Kong. All these, and many more, have lived their lives in the light of eternity.

Selwyn Hughes concludes his book *Heaven Bound* with this story:

Many years ago, on the East Coast of the United States, two ships passed each other – one a large sailing ship, the other a small steamer. The small steamer was just a run-down vessel that visited the ports on the East Coast, dropping off supplies such as tea, coffee, mechanical equipment and so on. The great sailing ship with its white sails billowing in the wind was a tremendous sight and the men on the small steamer caught the scent of spices and perfumes as it passed by. As was the custom in those days the captain of the little steamer picked up his megaphone and hailed the great sailing ship in this way; 'I am the captain of the *Mary Anne* and I have been out of Miami 12 days carrying little bits and pieces to the different ports. And I am on my way to New England. Who are you? In response, a strong voice boomed out from the megaphone on the other ship; 'I am the *Begum of Bengal*,

123 days out of Canton, having delivered perfumes and spices to many ports of the world, and now, homeward bound.[3]

We too are *homeward bound* and must ever keep in mind that, on the way, we are to spread the perfume of Christ's loveliness – into all our relationships, into all our activities and to everyone we meet – and this not just through one season, but through every season of our lives.

Questions for reflection

- How willing are you to go to heaven 'right now'? What makes you cling to earth? Try to be really honest in your answer.

- When you are facing struggles and difficulties in your life, what helps you to cope? Given that there are many scriptures that offer hope and comfort, try to draw together your own personal collection to encourage and inspire you in difficult times.

- Turn to Galatians 5:22, where the 'fruit of the Spirit' are listed. Which of these character qualities do you think God is wanting to develop in you at this stage of your life? How can you co-operate more fully with the Holy Spirit?

- What temptations cause you to become 'derailed' on the way to heaven? How might you guard against these dangers?

- Which of the helpful means listed in the section on 'How to "keep on keeping on"' do you need to cultivate in your spiritual life?

■ Is there a woman, or a man, whose life is an inspiration to you? Why is this so? In what ways would you like to become an inspiration to others?

Notes

1. *Heaven Bound* by Selwyn Hughes (CWR, 2003).
2. Amanda McBroom – Warner Chappell Music.
3. From an anecdote in *Two Years Before the Mast* by Richard Henry Dana.

National Distributors

UK: (and countries not listed below)
CWR, Waverley Abbey House, Waverley Lane, Farnham, Surrey GU9 8EP.
Tel: (01252) 784700 Outside UK +44 1252 784700

AUSTRALIA: CMC Australasia, PO Box 519, Belmont, Victoria 3216.
Tel: (03) 5241 3288

CANADA: Cook Communications Ministries, PO Box 98, 55 Woodslee Avenue, Paris, Ontario.
Tel: 1800 263 2664

GHANA: Challenge Enterprises of Ghana, PO Box 5723, Accra.
Tel: (021) 222437/223249 Fax: (021) 226227

HONG KONG: Cross Communications Ltd, 1/F, 562A Nathan Road, Kowloon.
Tel: 2780 1188 Fax: 2770 6229

INDIA: Crystal Communications, 10-3-18/4/1, East Marredpalli, Secunderabad – 500026,
Andhra Pradesh.
Tel/Fax: (040) 27737145

KENYA: Keswick Books and Gifts Ltd, PO Box 10242, Nairobi.
Tel: (02) 331692/226047 Fax: (02) 728557

MALAYSIA: Salvation Book Centre (M) Sdn Bhd, 23 Jalan SS 2/64, 47300 Petaling Jaya, Selangor.
Tel: (03) 78766411/78766797 Fax: (03) 78757066/78756360

NEW ZEALAND: CMC Australasia, PO Box 36015, Lower Hutt.
Tel: 0800 449 408 Fax: 0800 449 049

NIGERIA: FBFM, Helen Baugh House, 96 St Finbarr's College Road, Akoka, Lagos.
Tel: (01) 7747429/4700218/825775/827264

PHILIPPINES: OMF Literature Inc, 776 Boni Avenue, Mandaluyong City.
Tel: (02) 531 2183 Fax: (02) 531 1960

SINGAPORE: Armour Publishing Pte Ltd, Block 203A Henderson Road,
11–06 Henderson Industrial Park, Singapore 159546.
Tel: 6 276 9976 Fax: 6 276 7564

SOUTH AFRICA: Struik Christian Books, 80 MacKenzie Street, PO Box 1144, Cape Town 8000.
Tel: (021) 462 4360 Fax: (021) 461 3612

SRI LANKA: Christombu Books, 27 Hospital Street, Colombo 1.
Tel: (01) 433142/328909

TANZANIA: CLC Christian Book Centre, PO Box 1384, Mkwepu Street, Dar es Salaam.
Tel/Fax (022) 2119439

ZIMBABWE: Word of Life Books, Shop 4, Memorial Building, 35 S Machel Avenue, Harare.
Tel: (04) 781305 Fax: (04) 774739

For email addresses, visit the CWR website: www.cwr.org.uk

CWR is a registered charity – number 294387